CAVIARE AND CHIPS

"CAVIARE AND CHIPS"
Copyright © Carolyn King 2004

ISBN   0 9531860 2 4

First published 2004 by:

Printed in Great Britain by:

A little feast of poetry to suit all tastes – from the chronic chocoholic to the more discerning palate – each course to be digested leisurely, in the order in which it is served.

"Begin at the beginning," the King said, gravely, "and go on till you come to the end: then stop."
- Lewis Carroll ("Alice's Adventures in Wonderland")

———————

CONTENTS

BARTERED BRIDE

"Come, good sir, take this one;
you know you like her; right from the start
I saw that look in your eye
- there was an undeniable attraction.

And she's a good girl – probably
my favourite daughter. I don't want
to lose her, but the time is right
for you to take her. Do it now

while she's at her peak, unrivalled
by siblings or unborn sisters
not yet so much as passing thoughts
at the back of my mind.

I nurtured her for this; pictured
the day, the place, the look
on your type-face. Why should I grieve?
I've others like her up my sleeve.

Take her away to a page of her own
where the world can admire her.
I'll remember her first words, proud
to have given birth to a star.

When you've tired of her, don't forget
there are more where she came from.
Maybe I'll please you again, sir:
let me show you my poems!"

RESOLUTIONS

*(In certain weathers, Britanny Cross-Channel Ferries and P&O Liners sail very
close to the Isle of Wight. Last New Year was one such occasion.)*

Not something I'd expected:
to spot her limping home the morning after,
minus the make-up and bright highlights that I'd envied
from my bedroom window when I'd watched her
cutting a dash through midnight foam cartouches
strobe-lightly flashing in the inky blackness
as she set sail to see the New Year in.

Now, in the harsh light of a frosty morning stare,
she's just another weary vessel bound for port,
longing to hit the sack; hung-over as a cloud;
a pallid wavelet lurching pianissimo
and lapping in this wake-up-to-the-new-world
New Year; back to basics; struggling to retrieve
the flourish that was her outgoing signature.

I'd have imagined her riding the high seas;
toasting a champagne cargo; tilting at icebergs.
Better to live the dream than spend a lifetime
twitching the curtain, fearful of drowning sorrows
lest they return to haunt us on the morning tide.
When I embark on *my* voyage into the night,
I shall *fly* … and you won't see my heels for stardust.

FALLEN ANGEL

The view from our hotel balcony was always stunning
- and never more so than the night we dropped the baby.

(Michael Jackson had nothing on *us*!
I guess he'd be gratified to know
that he paled by comparison.)

You can have no idea how long it takes
for such a precious object to fall three floors.
From where I stood, it felt like drowning
- watching my whole life rushing by;
though as he was only one year old
I'm sure it was momentary for him.

Maybe we were distracted by the fireflies dancing
on the water; or, in a red-wine moment of weakness,
we held each other so tight that I lost my grip on reality.
Unthinkable! How could we let it happen?

As it happened, he landed in the bougainvillea
- petal-stained but intact.

In postcards home, we never mentioned it;
never spoke of it ever again; ashamed;
dumbstruck . . .   So, it seems, was he.

Sometimes I can't help wondering if all the words
he *might* have conjured fell out, just as he did,
on that star-crossed night – blown on the wind
before he touched down on the blossoms
that broke his fall – for, from that moment,
he broke our hearts with unbroken silence;
cold-shouldered language; never articulated a word
- as though his head was full of nothing
but hot air and a sense of unspeakable things.

He's seven now. Professionals come and go
- dumbfounded; failing even to scratch the surface;
rewarded by silent, enigmatic smiles.
He never makes a sound.

Somewhere, I've seen a classical painting
- "Madonna and Child"; the snow-white infant
kicking his heels on a scarlet cloth and smiling up
at his Virgin mother; blood-red brushstrokes
flowing like wine to crimson, revealing
the hidden depth of an *inner* wound
inflicted by my lapse in concentration.

Sometimes, in the hush of evening, I still see him
- my little angel! – red and rosy with health, snug
in the scarlet bracts of the bougainvillea,
smiling up to a whitewashed balcony;
safe in the arms of a surrogate mother
who seems to be doing the job far better than I.

It's the primal scream we'll never hear
in the deafening, muted silence
that makes me cry.

IRONY

After the pillow-cases are pressed and folded,
I iron her nightgowns:
the crisp, pink gingham with the roses
and the lace on her favourite blue;

till I come to the oldest; thin; translucent;
my fingers visible under the faded bodice
of phantom flowers and small pearl buttons
hanging on by a thread.

Then I recall how it used to be: vibrant;
bright yellow petals and lush green leaves
on fresh cream cotton; this before years of washing
wore it away to a shadow.

I love its frailty; hold it up to the light;
delight in the skimmed-milk whiteness; bury my face
in its flimsy folds, breathing the home-spun scent
of soap and water-softener;
shying away from words like diaphanous,
delicate, gossamer; searching for something
commonplace to express my feelings.

This is such stuff as dreams are made on:
lying in bed but flying on spin-dry
cool-wash-only wings;
it calls for gentle handling.

Later, packing her hospital suitcase,
I notice a single silver hair, wiry
as a fish-hook, caught on the threadbare fabric;
enduring as the ageing cloth to which it clings
- yet this so fragile: pallid
as a land-locked seashell, threatening
to crumble and disintegrate.

Odd, then, that I should be so unprepared
to find the empty bed, its white unwrinkled sheet
drawn tight by silent nurses, and the vacant locker
open-mouthed in shock.

Still more ironic my surprise when nightly
I detect an angel's pale form in a crease-free gown
suspended from a swinging high-wire coat-hanger
and shimmering iridescent in the dark.

———————

FOR JULIET

Seeing the sand in the car, I remember what fun we had;
hesitate, with the mat in my hand, reluctant to shake it away
- reminded of someone else who became a fanatic,
always insisting on sand-free feet
when the children ran up from the beach.

Not that it really matters,
for you can't get rid of it, anyway.
And when I'm winter-driving to work some pale-sun morning,
glints of gold will catch my eye and warm my heart,
like grains of friendship: indestructible.

BIRTHDAY WISHES

For your thirtieth birthday, you say you want a tattoo:
Buttercup*- a feisty character;
not exactly a feminist icon, but capable
– in spite of her childlike appeal.

I still cherish the memory of your nakedness:
the pale, soft skin of your shoulder
unblemished by birthmark or strawberry stain
- perfect in every respect.

Of course, I'll get used to it: just as I did with the earrings
(five in all - and all on one ear).
When the flesh healed, I actually grew to like them
- even to call them discreet.

So I smile and try hard to conceal my misgivings,
maybe thinking that Buttercup sounds a lot like you.
For *my* thirtieth birthday, I wanted a daughter:
I'm glad she has spirit.

*("Buttercup" is an animation character from an American TV series
– a "Power Puff" girl and something of a super-hero.)*

APPLIED MATHS

It was never my strength.
Even at school, I had no head
for figures: matters numerical
needed to be revised; he was the product
of infinite calculations.

Now he's a man, I see so little of him
that it seems my son has become a statistic:
.25 of the family unit we once comprised;
a further .25 being lost when his father
went on the rampage with a girl .5 his age.

That leaves just my daughter and me:
.5 of the original number.
So, you see, we find it difficult
spreading ourselves across the hole
where a round whole-number should be.

But we're doing our best to keep alive
the remaining .75 by letters
and phone calls (still including my son),
though as often as not it's his ansa-fone
we leave our messages on – he's rarely in.

Maybe my un-mathematical brain
has problems retaining the digits
or dialling them, adding a new dimension
to the sum of my wasted breath.
That's *his* story, anyway.

But every 25th of the 12th,
when I find his key on the rack
and know he's arrived in the night
like Father Christmas,
it's 24-carat 100% pure joy.

LABOUR OF LOVE

This is more stressful than childbirth:
I'm going to have a computer – my first.
And although, with my track record, I know
it's bound to be late, I'm preparing the bedroom
in readiness for the delivery date;

'cos it isn't just *any* old computer
- it's *mine* (I've been planning this day for years!)
to be cherished in bedroom (not cloistered in office),
the monitor keeping an eye on our progress:
a *personal* PC in every sense of the word.

And I know that Curry's think I'm absurd
to be sawing the leg off the dressing-table
to add a new corner for printer/scanner
to stand on. But, at the end of the day,
it's *my* PC and I think we'll be happy this way.

I'm ready; and butterflies in my stomach
remind me (again!) there's no turning back
- we're stuck with each other for good.
And I'm wishing that I was as sure as friends
who assure me it's sure to be fine;

for it's too late now: I've signed on the dotted line.
And I know there'll be times when I'll long
to make adverse comparisons of the new arrival
with "little Brother" – the manual typewriter
here by my side all along.

But when the teething troubles are over
I hope we'll establish a unique rapport
as close as a not-so-unsimilar one
that resulted before, when these same mixed feelings
attended the birth of my son.

And perhaps, in time, I'll come to acknowledge
its knowledge in areas I can't reach – accessibility.
For grown-up sons *do* outgrow their Mums;
and PC's, I'm told, can be serious fun.
But they don't write poetry.

WOOL-GATHERING

While I was still young enough to play the cowgirl,
riding the range and giving free rein
to imagination, they were the puffs of smoke
from Indian wigwams; though at heart
I always preferred Gran's definition: calling-cards
of little lambs who had gone astray.

Rescuing wayward strands of wool
from barbed-wire fences, we patrolled that field
of day-dreams, rolling the wisps of innocence
in our child hands.

Sometimes we watched the lambs from a distance;
but they were too timid to let us near
and the ewes too fiercely protective
to be ignored, fearful of predators.

Storm-clouds were never as far away
as we liked to imagine – threatening
to engulf the fleecy cirrus.

Now snags of wool are more brightly coloured:
scarlet or blue – like little girls' cardigans;
spotted by grown-up, professional hunters
and whipped away to Forensics;

while back at the ranch we flock to the school gates
- doting mothers, anxious as ewes
to ensure there'll be no straying of innocents;

for there are wolves out there.

SWEET CIDER

"But the apples are *green*," she protested.
And so they were! – even before he'd noticed
the blossom falling; or her teardrops
threatening likewise.

"Wait for the summer", he whispered.

High on his shoulders, she listened wide-eyed
as he told her they grew from a seed
and the little green striplings were too small
for picking: sour.

He'd been down that path before;
laying their premature dreams to rest
at the edge of an orchard:
the sister she'd always wanted.

Time to bury the past.

August would ripen the fruit: smooth, shiny skins
and round, ruddy faces with rosy-cheeked smiles;
like the pictures pinned on the nursery wall
- her paintings of favourite dolls.

Harvest came late this year.

Autumn fruition: he feasted his eyes
- mother, small daughter and child,
intent on their festival roles and immersed
in the fresh scent of pippins.

Counting his Midas windfalls,
he watched as his wife peeled the fruit,
exposing the white flesh, succulent
under its silky skin.

The baby took first place now.

But he dozed in the heady warmth
of the sun-kissed room,
dreaming of apples touched with gold
and the sweet taste of cider.

POEM

If you should ask me, "How is it you know that you love him?"
I'd say that if I kissed the top of his head while he was reading
my poem, I know he'd return the kiss between words;
and if his hand reached out for mine and I gave it,
he'd still go on reading; and if I nuzzled up to him,
instinctively, and his hand went further, fondling
the fluttering heart within my naked breast, I'd let him
know I didn't mind and it wouldn't matter;
while all the while I'd be half-asleep,
so that *he* might imagine that *I* might imagine it merely a dream.
Yet through it all I'd be thinking, "He has a wife:
this is quite wrong" – though, after all, we're only sitting together
(not even speaking) simply sharing a poem.
And if you should ask me what happened next, I'd think
for a moment and then say, quite truthfully, that I don't remember.
All I recall is an episode during which he never stopped
reading my poem and after which I never regretted it,
knowing we both felt the same and that when it was over
we'd smile at each other comfortably, as before
- just a little bit closer; and then he'd look into my face
and tell me softly, precisely, in depth what he thought of my poem.

LITTER LOUT

I always claimed that the clutter was down to the children.
After they'd grown up and gone - their father too -
things would be different.

For a couple of years while I sorted my head out,
putting my life back together, the house was tidy.
That's when the poems moved in!

Saturdays are the worst: just when I think my time's my own,
lazily looking forward to lying-in at the weekend,
they're up at seven;

nudging me; sneaking into the bedroom and creeping
under the covers, demanding I write them down;
even invading my dreams;

sheets on the bed, off the bed, flúng adrift all over the floor;
linen and paper and poems caught up in a pillow-fight
fill the air with feathers.

Some of them cling to my dressing-gown as I escape
to the kitchen; wheedle their way into unlikely places
- cereal bowls and bread-bins.

Then, as I walk up the hall, I find two or three more
waiting to welcome their pre-printed cousins who often drop in
through the letter-box;

litters of letters that clutter the doormat,
filling my head with whispered promise of joys to come
- the way all lovers do,

till the tables and carpets succumb to recyclable snow-drifts,
while sensible things like bills, bank statements and credit cards
lose the will to live.

But the house that was temporarily cold and empty
is warm and full; and I'm winning the losing battle
to tidy it up.

DUST TO DUST

Changing down the gears to second
and cursing the hearse-pace driver in front,
I realise Spring has arrived in the High Street;
catkins hanging like gold drop-earrings
over the wall of the funeral parlour;
birds-nest soup in the Chinese Takeaway;
garlands of pale yellow flowers.

Normally I don't notice these things;
but today I'm stuck in this sluggish procession,
paying a slow-moving tribute to the joy of living:
seeing life in a new light.

Lining the route, mourners are out on the pavements,
dressed all in black; some to attention,
giving a last salute; others dishevelled,
openly falling apart – so full of grief.

Now, regardless of Spring in the air,
the stench is un bearable: almost as though
they've opened the lid of a coffin.

Not that there *is* a coffin:
only some sad remains in a black bag
ready for on-the-spot cremation;
worthless, half-forgotten memories
scattering trails of ash in the wake
of the corporation dustcart.

Maybe I'm right to surrender my soul
to the poetry of decaying ~~rubbish~~ ... beauty
or maybe it's just a load of old rubbish.

19

CUTTING EDGE

At the edge of the meadow, where the cows avoid the wire
and the grass grows higher, he can lie
half-hidden from the ghosts of a guilt-ridden past.

Twelve years old and knows it all:
been there; seen that; done it.
But no-one ever bought him the T-shirt.

No-one ever bought him anything:
scrawny little figure, clutching the handle of a hold-all
and hoping for a kind foster-family to carry him off
in a Lord-won't-you-buy-me-a-Mercedes-Benz
to give him a taste of what it can be like
on the other side of the fence.

In fact, it was a Ford: but it felt like the answer
to a prayer. Not one of his – another thing
that no-one ever taught him, so he wouldn't miss;
like picture-books they never bought him. His instead
a grey multi-storey of unhappy endings
and the kiss of his father's belt.

Grass is exuberant – a sweet sensation;
cats-tail and cocksfoot foreign words and feelings
he's eager to explore, yet wary of the girl who tries to teach him
country magic – showing him the way to make the grass speak.

Raising his hands together, as in prayer,
he tries alone: places a blade of grass
between his thumbs and blows across the sharp edge.
Nothing comes: no strident screech-owl calling to its mate.
Maybe it's just too late to learn to pray.
Is it abuse to hope the grass will shriek?

He tries again: a sting of pain burns on his lip,
staining the sleeve that moves involuntarily
to stem the flow. He has no fear of blood,
transfusion, saline drip – wants just one thing:
to wash away the blot the cut has made;

> infinitesimal compared to the stigma
> wrought by another, even keener blade.

One day he means to lie in the grass, propped on one arm,
putting his hands together, palm to palm,
no longer needing to thrust them into his pockets
so no-one will see the scars upon his wrists.
One day the grass will *sing*!

THE JOURNEY

The first ten miles were the worst:
after that, she was reconciled to the journey.

Now and again he smiled encouragement;
touching her cheek; putting his arm around her.
Even the darkness failed to disguise his pain
as his sceptical eyes scanned the hummock
and travelled on over the stony ground ahead;
but they were always kind.

It wasn't something they'd planned:
nor was the journey. They tried to pretend
it was purely a holiday – time to take stock
in a mystical land where exotic birds flaunted
their plumage or flew low over the water
as gasping fish eluded the gaping bills.

One day they picked wild flowers
and he made her a garland of rue.

In ways it was like the honeymoon
they'd never had: quality time together,
sleeping out under the stars and dreaming
of easier times, the equivocal past behind them.
Some day she'd give him a child of his own,
no questions asked.

When they arrived, weary of travelling,
the city was throbbing with people
- her body with pain; fiercer than his;
all her own. Still he was there for her.
Later, nursing the child in the manger,
she wept for joy, the rites of passage complete.

He stood apart, holding back bitter-sweet tears
for the woman he'd always loved
but had never known.

READING STEVEN O'BRIEN

He comes to me like a stuttering child;
and right from the start I have a feeling
the things he wants to say are special.

Sentences break out here and there, but often
merely a couple of words are enough to ignite
the promise of fire. I draw the book closer,
hungry for warmth; he feeds me monosyllables
- and I'm moved.

I'm used to this: coaxing sounds
from the speech-impaired – children who know
what they want to say but lack the means.
He's something else: I'm the one with the handicap,
out of my depth on an open page;

speechless when the penny finally drops,
realising that what he's trying to say
is just too beautiful for words.

THE MAN WITH THE SHRUG IN HIS VOICE

He's as British as Betjeman's buttered scones,
unpretentious as "Housewives' Choice";
laid-back, self-effacing, good-humoured and fun:
the man with the shrug in his voice.

He reads with a curious, self-mocking tone,
and his vowels aren't hardened like Hughes'.
Reassuringly gentle, his quiet chat-up line
is incredibly hard to refuse.

It's not that I praise every verse he invents,
but I do like the way that he feeds them
to his audience – rather like seed-pearls to swine,
turning water to wine as he reads them.

For me, Simon Armitage sounds suicidal,
although I admire what he writes;
an air of depression makes even expression
of joy a mixed box of delights.

When he droned "Innisfree", Yeats (W.B.)
did little for its reputation:
in a tone kind of gruff, he huffed and he puffed
like a steam-train approaching a station.

So what has he got? – this soft-spoken man
with the smooth give-and-take line of patter.
It's the *shrug* in his voice, that seems to imply
"Take it easy – relax – it won't matter."

Now I've heard about frogs that get stuck in your throat
and you can have a flea in your ear
or ants in your pants: but what is a *shrug*?
The meaning, at best, is unclear.

The dictionary definition is brief:
shoulders raised in indifference, I read.
But there's more to *his* shrug – it can tug at your heart
like a dog with its eyes on its lead.

If it does have a life of its own, I suspect
it's a warm-blooded, soft-hearted thing:
a miniature Labrador puppy, a kitten,
a robin that's injured its wing;

a small, spineless hedgehog rolled into a ball,
disguising its long, lethal prickles;
or one of those furry brown caterpillars
who curl up on your palm till it tickles.

So it's somewhat surprising he doesn't succumb
to a stutter, a scratch or a cough:
but, though he's not Hardy, he's hardy enough
- a perennial known as McGough.

As for me, I'm told that the overriding quality of *my* poetry
(even when it fails to scan) is its degree of pathos;
which, roughly translated, probably means my poetry's
                                                    pretty pathetic.
I'd rather be known for a shrug . . . .

MOTIVATION

I write poetry to express my id:
or am I barking up the wrong chi?

SALUT!

We drank a toast in Fontaine de Vaucluse
to lovers: Abelard and Héloïse;
and wrote a poem, prompted by the Muse.

Our Provençal wine-waiter aired his views
on love and loving, shared his expertise.
We drank a toast in Fontaine de Vaucluse.

A local poet, aiming to amuse
inebriated tourists, tried to please;
and wrote a poem, prompted by the Muse.

That we were writers too seemed to confuse
his villanelle; he loitered with unease.
We drank a toast in Fontaine de Vaucluse.

He put his words to music – sang the blues
(sad lyrics fit for Revolutionaries)
and wrote a poem, prompted by the Muse.

Such company we hardly dared refuse;
he ordered three more bottles and blue cheese.
We drank a toast in Fontaine de Vaucluse.

We saw it was impossible to lose
this pixilated poet; worked in threes
and wrote a poem, prompted by the Muse.

Unlike the Bard, our trio failed to fuse
your Abelard, my Héloïse . . . reprise:
we drank a toast in Fontaine de Vaucluse
and wrote a poem, prompted by the Muse.

MISSING

Does she know he's gone? – I wonder;
the bare-faced moon whose searchlight sweeps
my bedroom through the midnight window.

I still miss *his* moonshine;
but I don't miss the Nile cruise honeymoon
he gave her, for I'd never dreamed the Nile
would be affordable on a pension.
And I loved our cheap hotel beside the Sorbonne,
so I don't miss his Île de la Cité apartment
with every mod. con. – though I'm sure it's great
and she'll make the most of lying in till eleven
(while I'm off to work at eight).

I hear he's into trendier exploration, too:
coached by his youthful instructor, he surfs the Net,
waiving his literary talents
in favour of purely mechanical functions;
selling out ABC for ICT.
Ours was the age of innocence:
passion professed by fountain-pen,
not processed by computer;
so I don't miss the transience of e-mails.

And I don't miss his moonlighting,
with its crescent of half-truths
and fabric of bare-faced lies.

What I miss is slipping into his shadow
when clouds disperse and hallmarked moonlight
floods the four corners of an empty room.

RIBES RUBRUM MIRACULUM

Someone said miracles don't grow on trees – we seek them out:
but I found mine by chance, beside the rhubarb patch.

It wasn't a classic miracle (if there is such a thing);
and if miracles happen only once maybe it wasn't one at all,
because this was there for the taking every long, hot summer
of my sweet redcurrant-jelly childhood.
Maybe that was a miracle in itself.

The burning bush paled by comparison; underneath
the currants, like the bronze sculpted figure
of a crouching child supporting a tiffany lamp,
I bathed in stained-glass sunlight streaming
through scarlet skins – transparent berries
whose pips, like unborn babies in the womb,
were clearly visible; every vein in the leaves
distinctly defined.

Kneeling now as I press the low-level switch
on the lamp, I'm back in that cottage garden
hideaway – incandescent reds and greens
from a sun-soaked umbrella mosaic re-inventing
those grapelike clusters of round, ripe fruit
and the brilliant essence of leaves;
blinded by colour and light, like Saul
on the road to Damascus.

But this is a rekindled memory – not a miracle.
Electric; while its predecessor was solar-powered
- and maybe a miracle after all; though if God
had anything to do with it, surely he'd grant me
the gift of tongues to describe it more vividly?
Simple words and primary colours are not enough
to convey such joyous psychedelia; something extra
is needed to sweeten the pill.

They were the exquisite colours of childhood,
those reds and greens of the redcurrant bushes
in summer sunlight; I dream them still
on misty mornings of middle-age, when eyes
don't focus so well and light is subdued.

I know now how much sugar it takes to make redcurrant jelly;
without it, even the plumpest, reddest, juiciest fruit is sour.

DEVOURING THE MAIL

Because I'm not one of those people
who can spend a weekend with an unopened letter
or eat my way through a box of chocolates
one at a time, I'm glad she sent me her book.

Perhaps I'm a natural glutton;
but chocolates never last longer than 48 hours,
and if anyone sends me flowers I don't have time
to arrange them the way I should.

Junk mail I can deal with: ignore it.
I'm equally equable about junk food
- take it or leave it:
preferably the latter.

But poems are like chocolates: one down
and 27 to go, all in compulsive succession.
So I'm glad she sent me her poetry book,
'cos you don't get fat on poems.

KAHLO IN VENICE

Reading his poem reminds me
of my first meeting with Frida.

Venice was sultry the night we arrived;
and there she was – stretched out
in St Mark's Square, bursting with colour,
her crimson outline the afterglow
of a sinking sun on darkening stone.

My daughter recognised her, and said
she'd introduce me the following day.

But dawn brought a rainscape
- tears in the wake of an overnight storm
that battered the city, striking its heart
with forks of lightning so cruel
that even *she* would have cringed.

We discovered the body – brain-washed;
wrapped in a sodden sheet flapping
against San Marco's rain-grey pillars,
the exhibition's address illegible
- wound round her slender neck.

It was midday before we located
the gallery; paintings vermilion
as fire-on-water Venetian sunsets;
 self-portraits - far more sedately dressed
than the artwork of yesterday's poster.

Now they've made a film of her story
and everyone knows how it ended.
I loved her best that first time I met her
- out of the blue, out of reach and offering
merely a hint of that unique passion.

REFLECTIONS

After a week in cypress-scented Tuscany
and silence broken only by the brash cicada,
this is like coming home: sea air and the familiar cry
of seagulls, swooping over gracious gondolas
moored to withstand the offshore breeze and rising tide
rattling their calm; staking their claim alongside
the Doge's Palace and the Bridge of Sighs.

Here in the Piazza di San Marco, territorial rights
belong to pigeons, grown fat at the hands
of camera-toting tourists offering grain
and photo-opportunities; while on a little bridge
in Calle Larga a long-suffering mime,
silvered from head to toe, stands smiling
on an upturned bucket, bowing low
and offering blooms to passers-by who patronise him
with their small-change compliments.

On the high Campanile, we feel the warmth of friendship
from sun-burned roofs beaming through terracotta tiles;
but winding waterways reveal *mementi mori*
– shabby buildings, flaking paintwork, ancient doorways,
sunken faces, grey, behind closed shutters;
features we depict from sheer imagination,
catching faint smiles like watery sunlight on our brush.

Home in England, through rose-tinted spectacles
distorting the true shades and shadows of its past,
we'll look back at coloured-glass kaleidoscopes;
but I'll still hold the image of a sparkling city's sinking heart:
a silvered mime smiling through faded flowers.

A DRAGONFLY TO DINNER

After a sun-scorched week in which our pallid limbs,
stretched out beside the pool like sliced-bread 'soldiers',
turn golden-brown from toasting in the Tuscan heat,
we rise; take up our sun-beds; and then walk
down through luxuriant Castellini vineyards
until we reach the burnt Siena road.

Breakfast at eight: English reserve begins to melt,
softened by rich Italian preserve – their *marmalata*;
sweet *miele girasole* – sunflower honey.
Licking our lips, we come again for more;
eager to taste the fruits of new horizons
as risen Lazarus to find his feet.

Over lunch, we guess at nationalities:
the energetic German with a French wife;
an Englishman who never speaks, but reads "The Times";
the blond Dane; each guest quick to guard his privacy,
elusive as the scuttling, lithe green lizards
hot-footing it across the courtyard stones.

So we are unprepared on this our final night
for miracles; scarcely expect to find the gift of tongues
among the antipasti – still less this intruder
whose coming fills the air with all-but-silent magic,
sporting no music like the brash cicada; yet we're aware
of some strange presence moving in our midst.

Flashes of blue and green attend the quick-fire dance
performed between the diners as a dragonfly,
the only creature of its kind that cannot walk,
captures respect and stirs imagination
with an impromptu, dazzling table-top display,
unnerving in its confidence and grace.

Almost as inexplicably as it appeared,
the uninvited guest, whose fragile netted wings
caught our attention like a shoal of gasping fish,
is gone; despite impregnable mosquito-nets
that seal the windows of the dining-hall,
barring last-supper strangers from the feast.

Dinner resumes, the visitation past;
but something memorable has touched our lives.
Maybe this solitary Tuscan villa
is closer than we thought to Galilean shores
where Peter, James and Andrew cast their nets
and hoverflies spun haloes in the spray.

When the dawn creeps through cracks on ill-fit shutters,
we'll pack our bags; begin our homeward journey,
heads filled with fly-by-night philosophy
interpreting the uninvited guest appearance,
lamely attempting a *raison d'être* that doesn't have a leg
to stand on – groundless as a transient dragonfly.

POST-HOLIDAY BLUES
(for Jo)

I'm learning to be alone all over again;
to think for one instead of two;
waking in the night expecting you
to be there, softly breathing
in the bed alongside; feeling
it's unfair that no-one's here
to share the memories trickling down
the pane of separation, like raindrops
on a wet Venetian morning
when old San Marco hid his charms
behind a cloud; wanting
to say out loud, "Remember this?"
or "Jo, it's eight o'clock: is it okay
if I open the shutters?
What shall we do today?"

Now dawn breaks with English birdsong
and I wake from dreams of Castellina
to an empty bedroom, cooler
morning air, missing
the throbbing beat
of the cicadas' music.
So "mi scusi" if I find it hard
sharing my thoughts with Little Q
and missing you.
I'll slip back to the old routine
in time, forgetting that it's not
the life I'd choose; happy
our Tuscan holiday was so sublime;
closing my eyes again
and dreaming of sunflowers.

MASTER-CLASS

We are at opposite ends of the learning curve:
you the high-flyer who's made it, straddling the upper point
of that crescent moon, dandling your legs between Heaven and Hell,
despairing of the bleak landscape spread out below;
I at the lower end, determinedly cheerful,
changing complexion to lift the spirit
like autumn leaves on a colourless canvas;
thoughts turning up at the corners
like a smile at the end of a poem;
a long way to go – and not enough time
for the journey – but ever the optimist.

If, in your wisdom, you finally plunge into the abyss,
maybe I'll catch you as you pass, snatching you
from the jaws of death on the tip of my chameleon tongue,
cupping my hands or cradling you in my arms
as I try filling your head with happy endings;
though I know you'd resent my interference,
for, after all, it's *your* life – and if you decide
to throw it away it's none of my business.
You're the one on the top of the heap, disillusioned with dreams;
and I'm the poor, silly cow still contemplating
jumping over the moon.

AGE CONCERN

This is the house where we dreamed red roses
and grew green salad   After he left,
the crop began to fail.
All that remains is the letters:
sad little bundles of faded leaves,
discoloured now – like shrouds;
even the rubber-bands have perished.

                              I'm not a gardener,
but they remind me of seeds, tucked away
in the inaccessible corners of envelopes
ripped open eagerly long ago;
some so shrivelled they slip through fingers
losing their grip; others still bursting
with plump expectancy, ripe for sowing.

Cradling them in my palm, I stroke
their pregnant fullness, half-believing
they still might grow – shooting out delicate stems
like tiny breach-birth limbs flailing the air;
newborn infants gasping for life
after lying so long in the dark.

                              Green-fingered friends
are full of advice: how to eradicate nettles
and throw dead wood on the bonfire.
I'm still lost in the lines of love-lettuce;
where would I find the strength
to dig over the soil – or the courage
to burn the dead leaves?

They're right, of course: it's beginning
to get on top of me. One day I'll lose the plot.
They think I won't know when it's time
to up sticks and bring out the dust-sheets
- probably laugh, wrongly presuming
I can't tell the wheat from the chaff.

But if you come again next Spring, my dear,
I might just surprise you:
perhaps I'll have moved to a new address
- a sheltered home, with a window-box
protected from the wind of change,
where I'll spend my re-awakening hours
growing born-again green-salad seedlings in the sun.

———————

FAMILY TIES

"Blood's thicker than water!"
was always a handy ploy
- especially when he wanted out.

Mafia madness:
when he was a boy,
he never questioned
family ties.

It was only later, full-grown,
that he told them
to get knotted.

SECOND SIGHT

*(In March 2002, advanced CAT-scan technology employed on the mummified remains
of Nesperennub, an Egyptian priest - 800 B.C. - results in unexpected revelations.)*

They gave him glass eyes;
probably to help him see his way more clearly
in the dark after his mummified body was entombed
and he embarked upon the after-life.
But the role of the shallow bowl at the base of the skull
remains unclear, less readily explained.

We're forgetting the fly-on-the-wall:
that other cat – the one they buried with him.
Watchful as Bast, she guards his secret
with a provocative half-smile that reminds me
of the Mona Lisa, knowingly implying she has all
the answers: *she* could tell us a tale!

But I don't think the bowl is hers,
for there's no milk of human kindness
in her destiny; she's just an onlooker,
sitting it out on the side-line.

Now it's *our* turn to smile.
Thanks to a 21st-Century CAT, we play a godlike role,
all-seeing; usurping the archaeologists' skill;
denying ancient historians their thrill of discovery.
We've no need to lift a finger – or even a bandage:
this is a more reliable way of discerning the past.

Glass eyes now belong to TV screens.
They cannot weep for us as we bear witness
to the daily bloodshed in the East – scenes from a land
he'd understand far better than his latter-day despoilers
who, with their high-tech methods, would have been
the body-snatcher's nightmare.

Maybe he *did* weep, lying in the darkness,
droplets diverted from those cavity cheeks
(for gravity is constant, irrespective of chronology).
I believe the bowl was there to catch the tears
flowing from those glassy eyes, behind his ears
and into the receptacle strategically placed below.

But, like those we've grown accustomed to disguise
as tragedy unfolds in nightly bulletins,
any salty tears he may indeed have wept
have dried up long ago.

SHADES

Last night (probably down to watching too much "Eastenders") I dreamed
my father was here; and somehow I didn't question it for a moment,
even though he seemed different from how I half-remember him.

This time, in the here and now, his hair was grey
and his faded blue eyes hidden away behind dark glasses.
I wasn't even sure that he could see me.

And I no longer plied him with dolls (presented shyly for inspection
on allocated days he visited); nor did I straddle
his motorbike – not that I should have expected to do so, as
- like him – it never recovered after the accident.

Something made me reach out – touch the bony arm
that was always in rolled-up shirt sleeves (just as a part of the engine,
to Mother's dismay, was always in pieces on the kitchen table).

Then, like a turned kaleidoscope, the pattern fell back into place,
summoning all the years of misplaced disaffection,
blending true colours into the sepia frame.

I never saw the longing on his face.

A STITCH OUT OF TIME

Sometimes, when the sun becomes complacent
on a warm June evening, I still sense her presence:
the little girl I almost knew.

I remember dark hair; and a dress as white as the page
on which I dare to write these maybe-memories.
I can feel soft wool against her skin
against my skin; and all the while the warmth
of early-evening sunshine lulling her, lulling me
into a dream of unreality.

Somewhere in this textured image there's a window;
curtained; muffling the ugly sound of traffic.
Inside, everything's soft and smooth and round;
except for the needles, clicking away like the hands
of a clock, while music curls up from the street
like cigarette smoke-rings, completing the Waterloo Sunset.

1967: and The Kinks are at Number 1.
But my number one is three weeks overdue;
and I'm so drowsy I'm almost half-asleep.

It seems I've been counting time for too long,
but it's too warm to put up a fight
or to move away from the cosy cocoon we've spun;
treading water; keeping the world at bay.
"You're not *still* waiting?!" – words that made me weep.
Maybe tonight she'll come . . .

But she never came: sent somebody else in her place
instead; and the dark-haired face at the side of the bed
was not *her* face but the face of my baby son,
as the Waterloo sun set slowly on some of my dreams
and I struggled to come to terms with reality,
loath to pass over my bundle of shattered illusions.

For the dark-haired child in the white woollen dress
was never mine: merely a face on a knitting pattern
- somebody else's little girl.
And it's so long now since I put down the needles
that I no longer possess the knack of communication
with someone who isn't there.

Yet sometimes, on a warm June evening,
words I used to murmur come back to me, in code:

sl1, k1, psso, p1;

and I snatch at memories, memorising snatches
of one-way conversation in cable and plain and purl.

She slips my mind for years at a time;
but I've never really perfected the art
of passing the slipped stitch over.

SCENTIMENT

Because it would have seemed criminal
to lock them away in the lounge at bedtime,
the sweet-peas are in the hall – their fragrance
dancing upstairs on ballet-shoes.

And tonight my mother is in the house:

my mother, the dancer, whose spirit still pirouettes
when the autumn sycamore sheds its twirling wings
and whose *Dying Swan* sank nightly,
whitely, like falling blossoms
on to the hall of fame's red carpet;

who never planted a flower in her life
but had more joy and verve in her little green-finger
than all the TV gardeners together.

So I bury my face in the velvet
of sweet pink sweet-pea petals,
breathing the perfume she loved and plunging
into a cut-glass sea of memories.

Later, from my bedroom door,
I look down on my childhood past
washed up at the foot of the stairs.

SKIMMING STONES

A regular city guy, he feels no empathy
for landscape – no fundamental need
for fallow field or spreading chestnut tree.

Born and bred just a stone's throw
from the outspread wings of a Liver-bird,
he's deaf to birdsong; naturally immune
to shorelines and horizons.
This is an island, far from madding crowds
and inner-city docks: he's all at sea.

Backs to the wind, we head down to the bay
– he and my daughter, I and my eldest son –
under the sturdy canopy of a million leaves
and a thousand branches eager to make him a part
of the picture, whispering words in foreign tongues
he can't translate;

till we come to a stone beach, cluttered
with crab shells and cuttlefish bones,
where we stumble on shingle, shale and slate,
crunching our way through Mint Imperials,
mini-Hovis loaves like those my mother buttered
long before TV's boy with bike and fresh-baked bread
struggled uphill over rough cobblestones.

And suddenly there are lemmings
let loose on the shore, hurtling their way
to the water's edge, grabbing at pebbles,
fragments of rock and flat slate stones
- sending them hop-skip-jumping out to sea;

while we, my daughter Jo and I, clearing away
the stranded seaweed, stretch out our limbs
and watch the talent show, commenting
on the style and distance of each throw
- basking mermaids caught in a time warp,
loath to let it go.

And the stones skim fast over shallow waters
- skilful surfers pitting their strength against the flow,
dismissive of incoming breakers
they can never ride.

I retrieve the discarded one
- a pebble with a hole in its side
like the lopsided grin on a chalk-face
drawn by a child.

I know that one swallow won't make a summer;
and one afternoon on an island shore
won't make a beachcomber out of a man
whose feet are set firmly in stone in a concrete jungle;

but here on my Island, perhaps for a one-off
breathless moment the force was with him
- and he could have slain Goliath, or skimmed
a stone that might almost have clipped the wings
of a mythical bird that roosts on a rooftop
but never sings.

POST-SCRIPT

Simon pinched my Mint Imperial!
Relatively immaterial, I agree
- it's just a metaphor: pity he
chose one I'd settled for.

Worse still, we'd a mutual topic:
stony beaches. Sad myopic, I thought mine
a unique image – on the line,
beyond the scrimmage.

All the same, *I* wrote it first
- scribbled scrimshaw, unrehearsed. Who said
great minds think alike? (Drop dead,
Carolyn – take a hike!)

S'pose I'll have to ditch my Muse,
send her packing: "Je t'accuse!"; serial
plagiarist the charge. Vox Imperial:
"Armitage Plage".

Maybe it's some consolation
we gave joint consideration to a line
so freshly-minted. (Only wish that *mine*
had gotten printed!)

RABBITING ON . . .

The mail-box is full of letters
and a hutch at the end of the garden
holds my syllables.

Sometimes the odd one escapes
before I've managed to cram it in
with the others.

Then there's a frantic chase to recapture
and soothe it into a sense of a sentence;
for runaway phonemes can spell disaster,
leading to echolalia
- or worse.

Here on the lawn, a few of my favourites
do enjoy comparative freedom
under the chicken-wire.

But even *they* need constant attention
to stop them from running away;
and nothing's more soul-destroying
than finding an over-excited adjective
racing off before you've a chance
to produce a proverbial lettuce leaf
or even a metaphorical carrot.

Maybe if I stopped to think about it
I'd be overwhelmed by frenetic activity.
But they seem to know
exactly where they're going
without any help from me.

At the end of the day
I'd be lost without them;
though they'd probably never miss me.

So I do what I can:
dividing them into lines;
taking away rhetorical questions;
adding some well-chosen commas
and semi-colons.

All in all, I seem to spend
a great deal of my time
trying to contain them
and keep down the numbers.

Though I know I can't win.
Because words are like rabbits:
quick to multiply.

MY BLUE HEAVEN
(March 2003)

In Qatar, where "nothing but blue skies do I see",
and the crystalline shopping malls are alive
with the sound of music, my taxi-driver offers a choice:
classical, pop or jazz.

And a smudge defaces the skyline,
like a tear from a blue eye-shadowed eye,
as I choose Tchaikovsky – his 1812 –
hoping the roar of its cannons will drown
the harsher, orchestrated sounds
of impending war.

GOING UP IN SMOKE

(20th March, 2003: the eve of war on Iraq)

This book is my inheritance;
and a premonition beyond belief.

Fatter than Tolstoy's, it reveals a personal story
of war and peace. The mottled cover disintegrating
under my fingers, it bursts at the seams
like a bloated, over-fed python sloughing its skin.

And tonight, it seems, the nightmare that started out
as a fictional fairy-tale is about to begin.

*   *   *   *   *

Whether it was cartophily or the obnoxious weed
that sowed the first seed of this vast collection,
I can't say. Both parents smoked. My father left
when I was five, taking his personal property away.

The album, somewhat slimmer, soldiered on.
I loved its cigarette cards, neatly slotted
into the soft, brown pages: Player's *"Dickens"*,
"Roses" by Wills, De Reszke's *"Kittens"*,

"Happy Families" by Carreras!
This was my favourite from the start:
even at five I sensed the hushed familial warfare
that threatened my childhood peace.

Strange, but I couldn't have looked at the book
for thirty years. When Mother died, I found it
in her cupboard; brought it home with me
and rediscovered the past.

As a child, I'd never remarked on the pages
that bore no cards; now I saw they'd been earmarked
for photographs – "call-up" memories.
One remained – an anonymous aircraft;

48

as for the rest – blank spaces, defined
by photo-hinges and briefly entitled
(in Father's hand) with mysterious phrases
- portraits of life in a foreign land.

So, while *she* left me her cigarette cards,
he left me the spaces to fill with my imagination:
clues like *"the largest unsupported arch in the world"*;
"Kalif"; *"old minaret"*; *"Hill Street, Baghdad"*;

"Moslem faith" and *"Tigris by air"*;
"Spent Coronation Day here ..." – *"... on this!"*;
"Baghdad Airport" and *"Baghdad West"*; *"Spot of rain!"*;
"Sandstorm"; *"Before ..."* and *"After ..."*

*   *   *   *   *

Spring 2003: twenty-six years since her death.
Peace talks have broken down: bombing will soon begin.
And Iraq will resemble the missing photos – spaces
instead of places: fading images playing hard to get;

while the page in the book will be blank as the look
on my grandson's face when I tell him Baghdad
is that empty space: it went up in smoke
and we haven't a hope in Hell of bringing it back.

It's lost without trace: nothing more
than the ash from a burnt-out cigarette.

EASTER SERVICE

Every April, as sure as eggs at this ritualistic time of year,
when his Spring-clean wife takes down the curtains
and hangs out the nets to fly in the face
of the holy Easter sunshine, he overhauls
his weapons of mass destruction.

Any remains of his last assault are condemned to the bonfire,
where billowing smoke obscures the white flags
of surrender; the washing grows grey-faced
and ashen – losing the battle, weary
of protestation lost on the wind.

Armed with his WD-40, he'll oil the wheels of herbicide;
service his B&D Rotavator, which mows down
innocents by the thousand, trundling it out
from its winter quarters (his DIY shed)
in time for the Easter parade.

The ammunition is stored elsewhere, under lock and key,
for he'll tell you he takes great care with pesticides,
germicides, slug repellents; besides, who'd ever suspect
that the garden's disused Anderson shelter
would hold such a lethal cache?

Sharpening shears and honing the spikes on the lawn aerator,
he sets to work with a vengeance – Delilah whetting her blade
on the stone that slew Goliath. Size isn't everything;
this is more practical than a stone
rolled away from the mouth of a tomb.

Now that it's gone up in smoke, he knows he's lost the plot.
They're treating his grandson for 75 degree burns
- a case of friendly fire; while the National News,
reporting events in Iraq, is followed at 6.45
by a "Regional Round-up".

Behind closed doors, his wife draws the heavy curtains
- still warm from her iron; he sits in the dark, haunted
by ghosts of a failed objective. All he was doing
was trying to keep down the weeds: he never meant
to destroy the Garden of Eden.

SPECIAL NEEDS

Adam's as high as a kite:
give him an inch and he'll take a yard.

He flies his carrier bag
(the one that holds his sandwiches)
on a long string,
the white paper fluttering
over the playground
like a ring dove – or maybe
his personal guardian angel.

Half-past-three and time to go home,
he's just coming down;

but the billowing paper-carrier
is still flying high above the school- yard,
tied to the stout iron railings.

Somebody must have given him
just enough rope . . .

Maybe his mother forgot to dispense
his Ritalin this morning;
or maybe it's time
to increase the dosage.

PANACHE

In between lessons I watch her
patrolling the corridor; trigger-happy.
After lunch she hides away in the Staff Room.
Sometimes I see her emerge, a hint of smoke
still clinging to her handiwork;
but I rarely see the moment of impact
- only the garish, crimson stain
that tells me she's hit the mark.

Somebody has to be there to keep the peace,
for schools these days can be violent places.
She has a steady hand – performs her duty
with unerring confidence, challenging me
to copy her style: not that I'd want to.
I couldn't open fire so blindly
- nor have the nerve to make the deed so public:
I wouldn't know where to begin.

Poised by the open curtain (for optimum daylight),
my left arm resting on the window-sill,
I finger the slim metal cylinder
as it glints in the sunshine,
rolling gently in my hollowed palm
like a tiny vessel at sea;
perfectly formed; encapsulating colour
- a smiling promise of devastating appeal.

Skilful in my own way, yet hesitant,
I take aim; but my tentative hand falters.
I'm not a Modernist: more comfortable
with an Impressionist's pastel shades
or multifarious palimpsests;
mixing the colours on my palette;
blending with subtle brushwork to outstrip
her pre-packed pigment.

For each dash of scarlet she applies,
I will experiment with three softer tones;
blot dry or powder over
until I'm happy with the finish
- texture, shade and sheen.
Nothing flamboyant: barely apparent.
Then, returning the mirror to its shelf,
I'll draw the bathroom curtain back again.

Maybe, of course, for her too it's a smokescreen;
the brash exterior brandishing the lipstick-case
a cover; the brave face she continually puts on,
masking her insecurity, merely an act.
Perhaps she takes her nightly curtain-call
glad that the show is over; wistfully
wiping the smile from her face; then welcoming
each perfect pale dawn with unpainted lips.

———————

SELF-SACRIFICE

I could have thrown myself into the sea
from the highest cliff – if I'd had the courage.
But, because Pisces is my star-sign, *The Sun* says
I must suffer the slings and arrows
of outrageous fortune, for the tide will surely turn
and in a couple of years I'll be riding
the crest of a wave.   I wish!

                                        Two years later,
here I am, still on the shingle;
holding out my hand to a herring-gull,
who nonchalantly takes it for a fish.

COLOUR MIX

Funny, the things you remember;
or think you do, till someone tells you otherwise.

So I smile at his memory of her red dress
on their wedding day, recalling serge
and the dull blue-grey of a winter sky
threatening Christmas snow.

All through the ceremony, she concealed
that inner glow; muffled emotion
under a warm wool suit and neutral gabardine.

Maybe it was the laughter in her eyes
that led him to imagine she was wearing red
- a contradiction to her Scandinavian cool;
more suited to exotic Indian art
and echoes of his childhood in the East.

Armed with the album, bursting at its seams,
I search for evidence – and find the photograph:
five of us on the register office steps,
cold as its grey stones under winter clouds
that showered confetti on his Danish bride
and winkled out a soft snow-maiden smile.

But wait! – A flash of colour takes my eye.
Maybe he's not so wrong: a dash of scarlet
brightens the sombre shades and mixed complexions,
like some precocious robin flying down
to steal the scene and step into her shoes.

This is the flame that burns so brightly in his head:
red leather – dainty footnote for a winter bride;

while *I* recall the sweetest part of all – when we
ended the day with carols round a Christmas tree,
toasting a new beginning that would never end
and singing of *another* love that never died.

SICK NOTE

Not the first time I've done it;
and pretty certain not to be the last.
Tickets bought, travel sorted,

suitcase packed
(even got a sitter for the cat!)
- I'm ready for the off; or so it seems.

Just one thing missing:
MENS SANA IN CORPORE SANO
(with the accent firmly on the latter).

"Never mind", they say,
"There'll be another time;
  it really doesn't matter."

But kindness can't contain
this singularly melancholy feeling
as I unpack my dreams.

WALKING WOUNDED

(A true story)

Maybe he'd been there before; so escape was easy.
Anyway, the Germans were after him.
So he walked unceremoniously
from the nursing-home and stumbled
into our summer garden, scrambling up the terrace,
braving the brambles, cowering from the spotter-plane
circling above, until he reached the top
and the old stone wall that overlooks the sea.
From such a vantage point, perhaps he thought
he'd have them in his sights as they advanced.
But night fell, followed by a birdsong dawn
of placid skies, quite bare
- and not a swastika in sight.

Of course, we'd no idea that he was there.
When the police arrived on Sunday morning,
asking if we'd seen an old man – frail, dishevelled,
recently admitted to St Joseph's, the residential home
around the corner – we feared the worst.
With his medication, they assured us,
he'd be well aware of his surroundings
and capable of knowing where to hide.
*Would he be physically able, then, to climb
the steep, stone steps?* – Mind over matter,
they replied: it's quite amazing what you can do
if you think it's a question of life or death
and the Germans are after you.

Sad, then, that they didn't have the foresight
to see the situation from *his* point of view.
Yes, indeed, he'd made it up the terrace,
finding himself a dugout in the bushes
and settling down to see the operation through.
When he heard the dogs and saw their handlers,
uniformed and armed with walkie-talkies,
panic struck: he fled – as best an octogenarian
could do! – into the long grass, farther from the path,
until the failing light and his own failing strength
combined to send him hurtling down the hillside.
That's where they found him on the Monday morning:
a broken man, resisting capture still.

Medical care mends shattered bones: the mind's
another thing – healed far less readily
by plaster cast or timely transfer to another home.
"They're everywhere!" he wept. "You can't trust anyone:
wish I was back in Slough – knew where I was there.
And, anyway, it's farther away from the coast
- no chance of a U-boat sailing across the horizon."
Matron said he'd never survive a move to London,
too distraught by change of any kind. Quite the reverse:
Asian doctors, African physio, Chinese chiropodist
and a Jamaican nurse . . . he's never felt so free.
This is the first day of the rest of his life:
and there isn't a sign of a German.

BALLETOMANE

"Mother!" we used to exclaim
as, to our everlasting shame, she *plié*-ed
and *entre-chat*'ed beside the bus-stop.

She was oblivious: one hand on the bar,
toes pointed in discreet anticipation
of a passing bus
or a *pas-bas* to the rosin box.

In her time she'd played them all:
Open Air Theatre, Regent's Park;
then, after years of classical ballet,
on into pantomime – "Cinderella":
Liverpool, Manchester, Birmingham, Leeds.
She was the belle of the ball
until *we* came along.

Children and show-biz tours aren't easy
to combine; so she settled
for bus-stop ballet and disapproval
from red-faced daughters, embarrassed
by such impromptu performance,
begging her to "behave".
She never could.

Now I explore her unbridled expression
through poetry, maybe hoping at last
to redeem my misspent past;

driving to cities whose theatres she played,
reading my poems
and, in a less balletic way,
following in her footsteps;

finding myself only the other day
passing a disused bus-stop
in the town that once was home.

What wouldn't I give
to bring her back for an encore!

THE IMMORTALITY
OF
DAISIES

An Elegy

Words are cold comfort in the fog of loss;
their clammy fingers merely chill the pain,
yet still they spring to mind – like seedlings sown
long years ago, promising life again;
though tears that fall upon a misted page
cloud such horizons, like unseasonable rain.

But when the sun breaks through, as break it will,
and when in time our eyes can bear to look,
those same few words may help us smile again;
daisy-chain-letters - tiny flowers we took
too readily for granted - re-discovered:
pressed petals in the pages of a book.

*   *   *   *   *

" . . . and loathsome canker lives in sweetest bud"

(Sonnet 35, William Shakespeare)

22.6.00. – 21.6.02.

A dream died yesterday.

It wasn't very old – just one day short
of two years, during which it grew
from a seed to a shoot to an arum lily
ready for picking – longing
to be picked.

I didn't nurture it
the way I should have done;
seldom spoke to it; kept my distance;
never caressed its leaves or stroked
the slender stem.

One day, when its beauty
took my breath away, I wrote a poem;
gave my instructions for sowing
like crossword clues or hints
on the back of a packet of seeds.

I like to think it thrived a while
before the petals dropped and leaves
began to wither; had no way of knowing
it would never see another summer
keeping the drought at bay.

Tears can't revive it.
Newspapers deal the final blow
in black and white, draining my life
of colour and my vision of tomorrow
and tomorrow and tomorrow . . .

This is the longest day.

DAY 1

I wake up with a feeling of unease:
2 a.m. – and the midsummer moonlight's
tarnished reflection in the mirror.

Then I remember.

The obituary churns
in the pit of my stomach;
I'm starved of dreams.

Eight o'clock – and more of the same:
a cloud blotting out the sun,
dulling my existence.

At work I'm bright as a button;
no-one would guess I'm hanging on
by a thread.

I come home to a mass of feathers on the lawn,
marginally outnumbered by attendant daisies,
and a fledgling thrush – whose huge blood-orange beak,
grossly disproportionate, pleads silent anguish,
opening . . . closing . . . opening . . . closing . . .
mute as a full-stretch python with its prey.

I've tried drowning an injured bird:
it merely revives the pain
and brings fresh wounds to the surface.
So we hold on till moonrise
for the final slump of nodding head
and heavy eyes.

Night falls late in June;
and, when it does, another light goes out
- beyond my reach.

Tomorrow, daylight courage will bridge
the yawning gap across the stairwell:
I'll change the bulb.

Tonight there'll be no gleam of comfort
under the bedroom door.
It seems appropriate:

even the house is in mourning.

DAY 2

The light-bulb is in place;

and now I'm trying to cut a perfect line
beneath four printed ones; aware
that my fear of heights is the reason
I'm trembling - it's nothing to do
with the after-shock of a bombshell.

But I wanted to do this well;

not that I need a reminder he's dead
- rather to re-live the moment before
I read the words: the silence
when the doodlebug stopped doodling
but love was still alive.

Because that's how it felt:

and now I'm one of the walking wounded,
shattered by the explosion – yet lucky
to survive the war.   I just want
a tiny scrap of the shell-case, to bring back
the bitter-sweet memory of 'before'.

DAY 3

On the third day he rose again,
thinly disguised as my son,
in a sepia dream about running
out of time: unfinished business.

Before the cock crowed thrice
I'd stumbled awake as many times,
struggling to come to my senses.
The image persisted.

I wish it had been about daisies
and a soft-spoken man reciting
his favourite poem – sailing
his virgin craft with natural ease
over the stormy seas of inhibition.

Now, when ocean-deep green waves
are flecked with white, I'll wish
they could have washed away
my indecision.

DAY 4

This morning I'm not dreaming.

It seems another dying bird is grounded
in a shower of feathers: not my sweet thrush,
whose dowdy brown besieged the lawn,
but a white albatross, its mammoth plumage
scattered across the churchyard on the cliff.

Torrential rainfall overnight (in June!)
has left the unmarked plot awash
on a sea of petals whiter than milk,
bigger than daisies, swept untimely overboard
from floral tributes - "Uncle", "Brother"
(none from wife or lover) - gracing the mound
I'd gone in search of late last evening.

Then it had looked so peaceful
- everything perfectly in place;
the new-laid turf at rest, resting
so gently over that gentle face.

But today we're down to the bare bones
of the matter, as limp petals cling
to the cadaverous frame - a thin wire wreath;
while all around fresh daisies, unperturbed,
keep silent vigil by the rain-swept grave,
their jaunty heads unruffled by the wind.

I pray it won't be long
before the ground can settle.

DAY 5

"Yet each man kills the thing he loves . . . "

So, despite misgivings (and the heavy rain!),
come next weekend I'll be involved as usual
in the daisy-chainsaw massacre, my lawn-mower
- this weekly-fixture substitute - sharp in attack,
while sturdy but defenceless white-strip players,
shoulder-to-shoulder, firmly stand their ground
and dare to raise their heads above the parapet
the instant that the final whistle's blown.

If Marie-Antoinette were here, she'd hand round
cake instead of half-time oranges; while I,
like Madame Guillotine, might try to justify
my occupation – making the point that innocents
are casualties in every war: the ends and means.
No life, however harmless, is insured.
And, after all, a daisy's not an individual
- merely a cheerful clone.

But a chainsaw is a mower is a sword.

DAY 6

Today is Barbara's funeral:
a dear friend – and another cancer victim,
yet twenty years his senior.
I'm weeping for two.

St Alban's on the cliff; high-church;
the grandchildren endearing
in cotton summer frocks, blue
as the sea is calm; the panorama breathless
as her final weeks – no soft breeze stirring
copper beech tree leaves, their summer black
timely for mourning after the springtime red
and still some way ahead of autumn green,
their unique colour scheme for once appropriate
- and sombre as the ageing congregation.

Communion is offered before the Nunc Dimittis;
the wine tastes sour.

It must have been the gardener
who cleared away the weather-beaten petals,
restoring order to that other churchyard.
He's here again – pulling up weeds –
as I arrive, bringing my personal devastation
for healing.   Feeling self-conscious,
I by-pass the faded wreaths, noticing
soft violet satin underneath the place
where huge white blossoms proclaimed "Uncle"
before "Uncle" withered away.

The heavy oak door welcomes me inside;
and on the font I see an arum lily,
green and white – the colour of daisies -
yet so different; delicately immaculate.

This is the inner sanctum where my thoughts,
given free rein, go galloping ahead as, kneeling
on a wine-red hassock, suddenly I find words
flowing sweeter than wine into the stillness
of the empty pew, where solitude
makes it easier to pray.

Do daisies die? – Even in winter sunshine,
I think I spot a few small sentinels
keeping faith between the headstones.
Certainly they seem to re-appear
as quickly as the mower mows them down.

Something inside me wants to lay
an arum lily on his un-trod grave.

But I'll probably leave it to daisies;
they seem to have more staying-power.
And, anyway, they figured in a poem
he read one day . . . .

DAY 7

And on the seventh day He rested . . . . ;
                    so shall I.
It's finished now:
nothing will change it.
Seven days more and we'd have met again;
instead, the printed word has made him
more of a fantasy than he really was.

Poetry's therapeutic:
I feel that in one short week
and a handful of poems
I've written him out of my life.
One neglected act has made it poorer:
I never even had the chance
                    to say goodbye.

AFTER-GLOW

Even in dreams, this wouldn't happen with anyone else;
but *he* is the exception to my every rule.

And in the morning I awake to grey skies
and the constant rain that greeted the arrival
of my daughter, many years ago,
my heart dancing for joy and skipping
over the puddles in the yard – untouched
by the incidentals of climate;
warm as a missed beat under the bedclothes,
glowing with consummation.

Just as before, while I've been drifting half-asleep
the milk has come – bottled up this time,
white through the rain-swept glass and gleaming
pure and perfect on the doorstep.

Over breakfast, it fills my cup
- full-cream and fresh as the newborn day.